Dictionary of Trade Terms and Construction Lingo

RYAN BRAUTOVICH

Copyright © 2012 Ryan Brautovich

All rights reserved. No part of this book may be reproduced or transmitted in any form or by any means, electronic or mechanical, including photocopying, recording, or by any information storage and retrieval system, without the written permission of the Publisher.

Printed in the United States of America

October 2012

ISBN: 978-0-9864404-3-4

"The only place success comes before work is in the dictionary."

~ Vince Lombardi

The Construction H.E.L.P. Foundation's Home Construction Audit program makes it easy and painless – through the use of our Home Building System – to understand how to build a home, how to manage your contractor, and how to protect yourself from being taken advantage of and scammed. We demystify the process and remove all of the contractor jargon to give you the building process in easy-to-understand, plain English. The Construction H.E.L.P. Foundation's founder and building expert Ryan Brautovich's exclusive 4-step home building system will ensure you are on the right track – and on budget – every step of the way. For more information about the Construction H.E.L.P Foundation, the Home Construction Audit Program, or any of the educational products, homeowner services, or construction seminars available in your area, please visit **www.HomeConstructionAudit.com**, or **www.ConHelp4U.org**.

A: Amp, amperage, amps, such as a 15A breaker.

AAMA: American Architectural Manufacturers Association.

AAV: Air admittance valve. One-way valve designed to admit air into the plumbing system during periods of relative negative pressure in the vent system to protect traps from siphonage and to remain sealed under zero or positive pressure.

ABS: Acrylonitrile-butadiene-styrene. Black drain pipe used to carry waste water (sewage) from the various drains in the House to a pipe known as the soil pipe. The soil pipe is located just outside the foundation of the House. ABS pipe is also used as plumbing vents through the roof.

AC: Air conditioning.

AC: Alternating current.

AC: Armored cable, a.k.a. "BX".

ACH: Air changes per hour.

ACI: American Concrete Institute.

AFCI: Arc-fault circuit interrupter.

AHJ: Authority Having Jurisdiction.

Al: Aluminum.

AMI: In accordance with manufacturer's instructions.

ANSI: The acronym for American National Standards Institute. This is an organization that tests building components and determines if the components meet certain prescribed standards.

ASHRAE: The acronym for American Society of Heating, Refrigerating, and Air-Conditioning Engineers. This Association establishes standards for heating and cooling, among other things.

ASTM: American Society for Testing & Materials.

AWG: American Wire Gauge.

Accessible, as applied to wiring methods: Not permanently concealed or enclosed by building construction.

Accessible, as applied to equipment: Capable of being removed or exposed without damaging the building finish or structure. A piece of equipment can be considered accessible even if tools must be used or other equipment must be removed to gain access to it.

Accessible, readily: Capable of being reached quickly for operation or inspection without the necessity of using tools to remove covers, resorting to ladders, or removing other obstacles.

Aggregate: A mixture of small smooth rocks; an ingredient used in making concrete.

Airbreak: A physical separation in which a discharge pipe from a fixture, appliance, or device drains indirectly into a receptor and enters below the flood level rim of a receptor such as clothes washer standpipe.

Air chamber: A pressure-surge-absorbing device operating through the compressibility of air. Expansion tanks have air chambers. Mechanical water hammer arresters have replaced air chambers in piping systems.

Air-conditioning: The process of heating, cooling, humidifying, dehumidifying, filtering, or otherwise treating air in a building. Most nontrade persons relate this term to cooling.

Air gap (for drainage systems): Unobstructed vertical distance through free atmosphere between the outlet of a waste pipe and the flood level rim of the receptacle into with the waste pipe is discharging.

Air gap (for water distribution systems): An unobstructed vertical distance through free atmosphere between the lowest opening from any pipe or faucet supplying water to a tank, plumbing fixture, or other device and the flood level rim of the receptacle.

Air handler: The specialized fan inside the furnace or air conditioner that blows warm or cold air through ducts to the rooms.

Alcove: A room or space such as a closet that is not large in relationship to the appliances within it. It would be less than 16 times the volume of a boiler or 12 times the volume of a furnace. For measurement purposes, only the portion of the room up to 8ft. above the floor counts in determining volume.

Alternative current (AC): Current that flows in one direction and then in the other in regular cycles, referred to as frequency or Hertz.

Anchor bolts: Bolts that hold the frame of the House to the foundation. Anchor bolts, also known as J-bolts, are cast in the wet concrete of the foundation during the concrete pouring process to secure the mudsill which is the wood framing member bolted to the foundation using the anchor bolts.

Antisiphon Valves: Valves or devices that prevent siphoning, typically by an opening to the atmosphere.

Apparent power: See *power*.

Approved: Acceptable to the Authority Having Jurisdiction (AHJ). UL and other testing laboratories do not approve materials; they test products and determine their conformity to published standards. Only the AHJ can approve them.

Apron: The small strip of trim wood that is underneath the windowsill. The windowsill is known as a stool in the homebuilding industry.

Arc-fault: An electric current propagated through air.
- **AFCI, Arc-Fault Circuit Interrupter:** A device intended to provide protection from the effects of arc faults by recognizing characteristics unique to arcing and by functioning to de-energize the circuit when an arc fault is detected.
- **AFCI, branch/feeder type:** A "first generation" AFCI device capable of interrupting parallel arcing faults. They do not meet the present code standard.
- **AFCI, combination type:** An AFCI meeting the standard for interrupting both series and parallel arcs.

Aspect ratio: The ratio of longest to shortest dimensions, or for wall, sections, the ratio of height to length.

Attic: The attic is the unfinished space in the House between the ceiling assembly of the top story and the roof assembly. The attic needs to be insulated over living areas and vented to allow proper air circulation from the House in the summer and winter. Most houses have an interior attic access panel, which can be located in the ceiling of a hallway, closet or bedroom, and allows access to the attic.

Attic, habitable: A finished or unfinished area meeting minimum room dimension and ceiling height requirements, and enclosed by the roof assembly above, knee walls (if applicable) on the sides, and the floor-ceiling assembly below.

Authority Having Jurisdiction (AHJ): The building official or persons authorized to act on his or her behalf.

BO: Building official.

BTU (British thermal unit): The quantity of heat necessary to raise the temperature of 1lb of water 1°F.

BWL: Braced wall line.

BWP: Braced wall panel.

Backflow: A flow of water or other liquids, mixtures, or substances into the distributing pipes of a potable supply of water from any source other than its intended source.

Backflow connection: Any arrangement whereby backflow can occur

Backflow preventer: A device or means to prevent backflow into the potable water system. These include air gaps, vacuum breakers, pressure vacuum breaker backflow prevention assemblies, and reduced pressure principle backflow prevention assemblies.

Backpressure: A potential backflow condition, created by pressure in the potential backflow source higher than the pressure in the water main.

Backsiphonage: Backflow caused by a loss of supply pressure.

Backsplash: A part of the countertop in a bathroom and/or kitchen (and sometimes laundry room) that is a vertical piece of countertop material connected to the wall. A backsplash is typically 4 inches to 6 inches in height.

Backwater valve: A device that prevents the backflow of sewage.

Ball cock: A valve in a toilet tank to control the supply of water into the tank.

Baluster: The posts that support the handrails, located on the sides of stairs. The posts where the handrails start or stop are called the newell posts.

Barge board: A board attached to the edge of a roof that projects beyond the wall of the House (also referred to as varge board).

Basement: A portion of a building that is partly or completely below grade.

Bathroom: In ASHRAE, a bathroom is a room containing a tub, shower, spa, or other source of moisture. A half bath contains only a water closet and lavatory, and is not considered a bathroom. In the NEC, a bathroom is a room containing a basin and another plumbing fixture.

Bathroom group: A group of fixtures including a water closet, one or two lavatories, and bathtub, combination bath/shower, or a shower. The group can also include a urinal or bidet and an emergency floor drain.

Batten: A strip of wood or plastic (usually 1 inch x 2 inches) that is applied to a roof to hold the concrete or clay tiles in place. Also, a batten is a strip of wood used to cover the joints of panels of exterior siding.

Beam: A horizontal piece of lumber that is used to carry part of the weight of the House. Beams are found at the roof, between floors, and between the basement or crawl space and the first floor.

Berm: A mound of dirt that is placed in landscaped areas to control the flow of storm water. Berms are also used in landscape beautification, to break up flat areas.

Birdbath: A condition where flat surfaces that are supposed to drain collect water in depressed areas called ponds.

Bird stop: A metal, plastic, or wood insert found at the lowest point of a tile roof (typically the round or barrel shaped tiles). This is to keep birds and other creatures from nesting in the underpart of the roof.

Bleed through: A term that describes a material that passes through another material and generally discolors the second material. An example of bleed through is redwood and cedar wood sap (tannins) that bleed through paint. It can also apply to rust from nails and staples that bleed through stucco.

Blocks: Blocks are pieces of wood installed at the ends (and sometimes at intermediate points) of floor joists, as to prevent the joists from twisting. By the use of blocks, the floor joists are tied together to create a more rigid component. Blocks are also found where floor joists lap one another (the joists cannot span the entire distance so a lap is created). Blocks are also used between studs to serve as a firestop. The blocks are typically made from the same material as the joists or the studs.

Bonded, bonding: Connected to establish continuity and conductivity.

Bonding jumper: A conductor installed to electrically connect metal gas piping to the grounding electrode system.

Braced wall line (BWL): A straight line through the building plan representing the location of lateral resistance provided by wall bracing.

Braced wall panel (BWP): A full-height section of wall designed to resist shear forces by application of bracing materials.

Branch: Any part of the drains except a main, riser, or stack.

Branch circuit: The circuit conductors between the final OCPD (breaker or fuse) protecting the circuit and the outlet or outlets.
- **Branch circuit, general purpose:** Branch circuit that supplies two or more receptacles or outlets for lighting and appliances.
- **Branch circuit, individual:** Branch circuit supplying only 1 piece of equipment.
- **Branch circuit, multiwire residential:** Branch circuit consisting of 2 hot conductors having 240V potential between them and a grounded neutral having 120V potential to each hot conductor.
- **Branch circuit, small appliance:** Branch circuit supplying portable house-hold appliances in kitchens and related rooms and that has no permanently installed equipment connected to it.

Branch Interval: A vertical measurement of distance, at least 8ft, between connections of horizontal branches to a drainage stack, measured down from the highest horizontal branch connection.

Branch vent: A vent connecting two or more individual vents with a vent stack or stack vent.

Breaker: A specialized switch found inside a panel (usually gray and known as a breaker panel) that will interrupt the flow of electricity in the event of a short circuit or an electrical surge. The act of interrupting is called "tripping". The small handle of a tripped breaker will be in the middle position between the markings OFF and ON. A tripped breaker will have to be turned off before it can be reset to the ON position. Breakers are usually found in groups in the panel and they are labeled as to which circuits they control.

Brow ditch: A ditch that sits on top of a retaining wall. It is designed to keep surface water from flowing behind and over the wall.

Building drain: The lowest piping of a drainage system that conveys discharge of soil, waste, and drainage pipes in the building to the building sewer beginning 30in (24in in UPC) outside the building wall.

Building Official: The person who is the lead of the local department that issues building permits. This is usually a county or city agency. Building Officials, through their deputies, perform inspections and enforce the various Building Codes.

Building paper: A specially made thick paper that is stapled to the outside of the frame of the House. Building paper is used prior to application of the exterior finish material (such as stucco, wood siding, shingles, etc.) The paper is impregnated with a substance during its manufacturing process that makes it resistant to the flow of moisture. If the stucco or siding leaks, the building paper will serve as a secondary backup to prevent moisture from getting into the walls.

Building sewer: Horizontal piping from a drainage system extending from the building drain to public or private sewer or private sewage disposal system.

Building thermal envelope: The basement walls, exterior walls, floor, roof, and other building elements that enclose conditioned space.

Bull nose: A piece of material that projects slightly past the supporting material and is rounded at its outer edge. Bull nosepieces can be found on roofing, interior trim, stair tread and countertops and "finish off" a flat surface.

CATV: Cable television.

CFM: Cubic feet per minute.

CMU: Concrete masonry unit.

CO: Carbon Monoxide or Cleanout.

CPVC: Chlorinated PVC pipe.

CSST: Corrugated stainless steel tubing for gas.

CU: Copper.

CW: Clothes washer.

CW&V: Combination waste & vent.

Capillary action: The act of drawing a liquid, usually water, into another material. A good example of this is a sponge absorbing water. In the building industry, water can be drawn up into wood, stucco, or concrete by capillary action.

Casing: Known as trim pieces that will finish off an opening. Most commonly found at door openings and mistakenly called frames, but castings can also be found around windows and shadowboxes.

Caulk: A gooey material that is used to seal joints for the purpose of keeping water out. Caulk is usually found around bathtubs and is applied with a tool known as a caulking gun. There are many different types of caulks for various uses. It is critical to use the correct variety of caulk product for each situation.

Cement: A term that has been mistakenly interchanged with the word concrete, but in fact is one of the ingredients of concrete. Cement is the "pasts" that will bind sand and aggregate together. Because of its chemical composition and alkalinity, cement can burn the human skin.

Central-fan-integrated supply system: A method of supplying whole-house ventilation through a makeup air duct connected to the supply ducts of a forced air system and a timer on the furnace fan control.

Chain drive: The mechanism that opens and closes the garage door and is part of the automatic garage door opener. These automatic garage door openers operate with three types of drives, either chain drive, screw drive, or belt drive.

Chase: A chase is a horizontal or vertical box in which a flue pipe, generally a chimney flue, is located. The chase is built around the flue and it extends above the roofline by an amount specified in the Building Code. Chases can also contain plumbing pipes or wiring.

Check valve: A device used to prevent the flow of liquids in a direction not intended in the design of the system. Check valves are not backflow preventers. They are often used in solar systems.

Chimney: A primarily vertical structure containing one or more flues, for the purpose of carrying gaseous products of combustion and air from an appliance to the outside atmosphere. Factory-built chimneys must be listed and labeled. Masonry chimneys are field-constructed of solid masonry units, bricks, stones, or concrete.

Chimney connector: A pipe connecting a fuel-burning appliance to a chimney flue.

Cleanout: An opening in a plumbing waste line to allow access to the piping for the purpose of inspection and cleaning. Cleanouts are required by the plumbing codes and are typically found beneath kitchen sinks and just outside the foundation of the House.

Closed loop system: Any system that uses the same fluid or gases over and over and is returned to the source for heating or cooling.

Closet: See "Alcove".

Clothes closet: A non-habitable room or space intended primarily for storage of garments & apparel.

Coffered ceiling- A ceiling that is not flat but has a portion of it lifted up to create a more dramatic architectural effect. The lifted portion is usually found in the middle of the ceiling.

Combination waste drain & vent system: A system employing horizontal and/or vertical pipes functioning as vents and drains for sinks and floors by providing for free movement of air above the water line in the horizontal pipe. CW&Vs are not self-scouring and their use is restricted.

Combustible material: Any material not defined as noncombustible. The extent of combustibility of surface materials is measured in flame spread index and smoke-developed index. Many HVAC components require specified clearances from combustible material, including the paper facing of gypsum board.

Combustion air: Air required for combustion of a fuel. It includes that air that is burned with the fuel, air for dilution of the flue gases and that is introduced into draft hoods, and ventilation air that cools appliances.

Common area: Refers to areas that are owned in common by all members of a homeowners association. This term is associated with condominium projects and is planned unit developments and may include such items as the exterior of buildings, landscape, driveways, recreation facilities and mailboxes. Common areas usually have their own legal description located in the deed to the condominium or individual lot, as applicable.

Common vent: A pipe venting two trap arms on the same branch, either back to back or one above another.

Compaction- An engineering term given to the degree of tightness of the soil around and under the House or behind a retaining wall. The soil under the foundation must achieve a certain degree of compaction before the foundation can be poured. Driveways, patios and walkways should be poured on compacted soil. Uncompacted soil is often referred to as native soil or loose soil.

Compressor: A motor driven pump that compresses a gas as part of the air conditioning process.

Concealed: Not exposed to view without removal of building surfaces or finishes.

Concrete: A mixture of sand, gravel (sometimes called aggregate) and cement. This mixture becomes concrete when it is mixed with water and is allowed to cure.

Condensate line: The plastic or metal pipe that comes out of the air conditioning part of the furnace. Condensate lines conduct water from the air conditioner coil to the outside of the House or to a trap.

Condominium: Buildings, parts of which are owned in common with other people. This is a legal term and is often confused with an architectural style. Condominiums can include townhouses, flats and even detached homes, so long as part of the project is owned in common by all of the owners of the project.

Confined space: A room or space having a volume less than 50 cu. ft. for each 1,000 Btu input rating of all fuel-burning appliances in the room or space.

Connector: A device such as a joist hanger, post base, hold-down, mudsill anchor, or hurricane tie used to connect structural components.

Contamination: Impairment of potable water quality that creates a health hazard.

Continuous waste: A drain from two or more adjacent fixtures connecting the compartments of set a set of fixtures to a trap or connecting other permitted fixtures to a common trap. An example is a double kitchen sink with each side connecting together and then to the trap.

Control joint: A linear separation made during the pouring of concrete (or stucco in the case of the installation of an expansion joint) made by troweling with a v-shaped tool. Its purpose is to provide a slightly weaker spot in the concrete so it will crack along the joint. The joint can also be a groove made with a concrete saw at least one day after the concrete is finished.

Controller: A device to directly open and close power to a load.

Corbel: A bracket having at least two sides at right angles and often ornately carved. This bracket may support a shelf or an element that projects out from a House such as a bay window or a fireplace mantel.

Corner bead: A corner bead is a long strip of material that is applied vertically to "finish off" a corner. The corner may be a drywall corner or a stucco corner. Corner beads are usually made of metal, including wire, and sometimes are even made of stiff paper.

Counter-flashing: Metal flashing that fits up under the visible flashing on roofs, around chimneys and windows.

Crawl space: This is the space between the soil and the underside of the first floor joists. It is found in houses that have a pier and grade beam foundation, and do not have a basement. The Building Codes specify the minimum height of the crawl space.

Cricket: A section of the roof that is often found between the roof and a vertically projecting structure, such as a chase. The cricket is constructed to deflect water away from the chase, where the chase and the roof meet. This is so that water does not accumulate and leak into the House.

Cripple wall: Wood-framed wall extending from the foundation to joists below the first floor. Found in the underfloor area.

Cross-Connection: A backflow connection or other arrangement whereby a potable water system may be contaminated.

Crowning: A condition usually applied to wood, often hardwood floors, where the wood takes on moisture and the center portion of the board becomes higher than the edges. The opposite of cupping. This condition can also apply to floor joists, where the center of the joist becomes higher than the ends.

Crown molding: A decorative architectural trim piece made of wood, plastic, plaster, or foam that covers the intersection of walls and the ceilings.

Crown weir (trap weir): Highest point of the inside portion of the bottom surface of the horizontal waterway at the exit of a trap. Water flows into the trap arm once it rises above the crown weir.

Cupping: A condition that occurs when boards (including flooring) dry unevenly and the edges become higher than the center.

Cure: The act of a building material drying out and coming to equilibrium with its surroundings. A good example of curing is concrete. Concrete cures from the initial placement as it dries out. In the first three days concrete is very weak and after 28 days concrete, when properly mixed, is said to reach 90% of its maximum strength. Other materials that cure are stucco, paint, deck coatings and fireplace linings.

DC: Direct current.

DFU: Drainage fixture unit.

DW: Dishwasher.

DWV: Drain, waste & vent.

Damper: A hinged flap of metal found above the firebox in fireplaces to close off the flue to warm air escaping from the room when there is no fire. The damper must be open when using the fireplace. It also prevents wind from blowing down the chimney when it is not in use. Dampers are also found in the ducts of heaters and exhaust fans.

Dampproofing: A coating intended to protect against the passage of water through walls or other building elements. It is a lesser degree of protection than waterproofing.

Daylight: A term given to a condition where a covered or buried object protrudes through its cover and becomes visible. An example is the visible end of a buried pipe—at the point where the pipe becomes visible, it is said to have "daylighted".

Dead load: The weight of all materials of the building and fixed equipment.

Dead nuts (slang): Having all the required or desirable elements, qualities, or characteristics; as good as it is possible to be.

Decorative appliance for installation in fireplaces: An assembly with artificial logs and with gas burners to simulate a solid-fuel fire, and installed inside a fireplace otherwise capable or burning solid fuel. They can be either manually or automatically operated. If automatic, they must include a flame safeguard device.

Decorative shroud: A partial enclosure for aesthetic purposes that surrounds or conceals the termination of a chimney or vent. Decorative shrouds must be specifically listed for the chimney or vent assembly and are often installed incorrectly.

Derating: A reduction in the allowable ampacity of conductors because of ambient temperatures >86°F or more than three current-carrying conductors in the same raceway, or for cables without spacing between them.

Developed length: The distance measured along the centerline of a pipe.

Device: A piece of equipment that carries or controls electrical energy as its primary function, such as a switch, receptacle, or circuit breaker.

Diaphragm: A horizontal or nearly horizontal system, such as a floor, acting to transmit lateral forces to the vertical resisting elements.

Dilution air: Air that combines with flue gasses at the draft hood of an appliance. See "combustion air".

Direct-vent appliances: Appliances that are constructed and installed so that all air for combustion is derived from the outside atmosphere and all flue gases are discharged directly to the outside atmosphere, usually by a coaxial flue pipe inside the combustion air pipe.

Directional fittings: Drainage fittings designed to join two pipes and direct their flow, such as wyes, combos or tees with baffles.

Discharge pipe: A pipe that conveys the discharge from a fixture or plumbing appliance.

Displacement: Refers to any horizontal or vertical movement of a building or the component within. More frequently it is used to describe the settlement or the heave of a foundation and the settlement of utility trenches that were once level with their surroundings.

Door: A movable structure used to close off an entrance to a room, building or covered enclosure, consisting of a panel of wood, glass or metal or other various building materials. An entire glossary could be written about doors, but here is a condensed version:

- **Exterior Door:** Any door that is on the outside wall of a House. The door has been manufactured to be weather resistant subject to proper maintenance.
- **Fire rated door:** A door that has been rated by an independent laboratory and has a label attached setting forth its rating. These doors can be made of many materials including wood, fiberglass, steel and composite wood material. A 20 minute fire rated of 1 3/8 inch solid core door is generally required to be placed between the garage and House and sometimes the entrances to condominium homes. The rating usually states that the door will withstand a fire for a certain number or minutes.
- **Flush door:** A door or series of doors that are hinge mounted (as opposed to a patio door that moves on tracks) and provides access to a courtyard, patio or garden. French doors are often found with divided lites (small panels of glass in individual frames as opposed to one large panel). May be used as interior doors between rooms.

- **Hollow core door:** Refers to the method of construction of that door. These doors have airspace between the front panel and the back panel of the door. The airspace between the front and back panel often contains a cardboard "honeycomb" inside.
- **Interior door:** Any door that is found inside the House and may include doors from one room to the other as well as cabinet doors.
- **Overhead door:** Also known as the garage door. May be constructed as a one-piece door or may be constructed in sections. A sectional door rides up into the garage ceiling on tracks whereas the one-piece door operates with springs and hinges.
- **Patio door:** An exterior door that is usually comprised of two panels, one sliding and one stationary. Patio doors are also known as sliding glass doors.
- **Pocket door:** A door that does not swing in or out, but slides across the opening from a "pocket" inside the wall.
- **Raised panel door:** A door that is manufactured with panels either individually inserted into the door or embossed into the face of the door as part of the manufacturing process. Raised panel doors can be solid core or hollow core.
- **Shower door:** The glass or plastic door that permits access to the shower.
- **Solid core door:** A door that has no airspace between the front and back panel, but is instead solid wood or some material that is glued or laminated to the front and back panels. Used in exterior applications and more custom interior applications.

Doorstop: The piece of trim that is put around three sides of a door jamb to stop the movement of the door when it is closed and sometimes to provide a rudimentary seal for light, noise and air.

Downspout: A specialized pipe usually made of aluminum, galvanized steel or plastic that runs from the roof gutter opening down the wall to the ground.

Draft: The flow of gases or air through a chimney or flue caused by pressure differences. An induced draft appliance has a fan to overcome the resistance of the combustion chamber while still delivering flue gas to the vent at non-positive pressure relative to the atmosphere. A forced draft appliance delivers flue gas under positive pressure. Natural draft is caused by the height of the chimney and the difference in temperature of hot gases and outside atmosphere.

Draft Hood: A nonadjustable device integral to an appliance or made part of the appliance connector. It provides for the escape of flue gases from the appliance in the event of insufficient draft, backdraft, or stoppage. A draft diverter (typical on water heaters) prevents backdraft from entering the appliance and neutralizes the stack effect on the operation of the appliance.

Draft regulator: A device that functions to maintain a desired draft in the appliance by automatically reducing the draft to the desired value. These are usually adjustable, such as the barometric damper on an oil-burning appliance flue. A double-acting barometric draft regulator is free to move in either direction and protect against both excessive draft (that could allow the flame to lift) and backdraft.

Draftstop: Material that is inserted into a wall to limit the spread of fire and smoke. Frequently used materials are wood, drywall, insulation and masonry block. Draftstops are also found in chimney chases and between floors of multi-story condominium units. They are usually made of sheetmetal.

Drain:
- **Deck drain:** A drain located in a patio or elevated deck to control and direct rainwater in that area.
- **French drain:** Similar to a trench drain, but there is no pipe at the bottom of the trench.
- **Overflow drain:** An overflow drain protects the structure in the event that the main drain plugs up. The overflow drain is typically two inches higher than the main drain. Overflow drains are also found on bathtubs and lavatory sinks.
- **Plumbing drain:** Any drain that is found at the low point of the plumbing fixture, such as a bathtub, shower, sink, etc.
- **Roof drain:** Any drain that drains the roof area including the hole in the gutter. If the drain is ad the edge of a flat roof, it is called a scupper.
- **Trench drain:** A drain often located in a yard or hillside area that consists of a trench with a perforated pipe at the bottom and gravel filled on the top. The term is incorrectly interchanged with French drain.
- **Yard drain:** Also known as an area drain or a site drain. This drains rainwater and irrigation run-off from landscaped areas.

Drainage fixture unit: A value used to calculate a fixture's load on the drainage system.

Drainage system: Includes all the piping within public or private premises, which conveys sewage to a legal point of disposal.

Drain, waste, and vent: The system of piping and fittings that carries drainage, waste, and sewer gases and that equalizes atmospheric pressure at traps to protect the occupants from the contaminated gases in the system.

Draw: The ability of a flue, chimney, or vent to pass air, smoke, or other vapors from the bottom up and out the top. Unless impeded by some source, all vertical tubes have a natural draw due a difference in atmospheric pressure.

Drip irrigation: A method of irrigating plants, shrubs and trees with low pressure, low volume piping and tubing system. The advantage of drip irrigation is that it significantly conserves water compared to conventional methods of irrigation.

Driveway: See Flatwork.

Dry rot: Refers to a condition of rotting, usually wood but sometimes paper and drywall when the material is wetted repeatedly and dries between wettings. Wood that is dry rotted is internally infected by a fungus. The wood will often look almost in its original form, but it will have no structural value and can be easily pieces with a screwdriver.

Drywall: A gypsum based panel that is nailed or screwed to the studs that makes up the interior wall of the house. These panels are also known as Sheetrock. Drywall derives its name from being a dry process as opposed to the wet lath and plaster process that was used years ago to finish off interior walls. Drywall is typically finished by placing tape over the panel joints and applying drywall compound, known as taper's mud, and finishing the process by spraying or troweling drywall texture onto the wall.

Dual pane: A term applying to the construction of a window skylight or patio door. Dual pane means that there is an outside layer of glass and an inside layer of glass separated by a spacer up to 5/8 inch in thickness and a dead air space between the two panes of glass. This is sometimes called insulating glass.

Duct: A continuous passageway for the transmission of air (usually forced) made of factory-built components.

Dutch gutter: A rainwater diverter found on roofs, often over doorways or where the placement of a conventional gutter is impractical. It is usually inserted between row of shingles or tile, and it protrudes up above the roofline by about three or four inches.

e.g.: For example (exempli gatia).

EGC: Equipment grounding conductor.

EIFS: An acronym standing for Exterior Finish Insulating System. This component system, when applied to the exterior of a House, consists of building paper, foam insulation, wire mesh (lath) and synthetic stucco product.

EMT: Electrical metallic tubing.

ENT: Electrical nonmetallic tubing, a.k.a "Smurf tubing".

ERV: Energy-recovery ventilator.

EV: Electrical Vehicle.

EXC: Exception to rule will follow in the next line.

Eave: The underside of a section of the roof that extends past the walls of House.

Effective opening: The cross-sectional area of a water outlet, expressed in terms of the diameter of an equivalent circle. In the case of a faucet, measured at the smallest orifice or in the supply piping.

Efflorescence: White powdery material that appears on the surface of concrete and stucco as the drying out proves occurs. Wet winter weather may cause concrete and stucco to effloresce.

Elastomeric: A term given to coatings that have "stretch" characteristics and are applied to many decks and low- pitched roofs. Elastomeric components are mixed together and applied with trowels or rollers. Several coats are applied and if the surface is to be walked upon, often sand, pebbles or crushed walnut shells are applied in the final coat. Some elastomeric paints are made to be applied stucco.

Energy-recovery ventilator : Same as "heat-recovery ventilator" with a heat exchanger core that removes humidity. ERVs require a drain to remove water that condenses in them.

Equipment: A general term including materials, fittings, devices, appliances, luminaires (fixtures), apparatus, machinery, and the like used as a part of, or in connection with, an electrical installation.

Equipment Grounding Conductor (EGC): A wire or conductive path that limits voltage on metal surfaces and provides a path for fault currents.

Escutcheons- a piece of trim, chrome, brass, plastic or wood that is used to finish off the area of penetration of a pipe through a wall or ceiling. They are usually round and one inch to three inches in diameter.

Evaporative cooler: A device used for reducing the sensible heat of air for cooling by the process of evaporation of water into an airstream. Also known as a "swap cooler." Evaporative coolers are used in hot, dry climates, and also for makeup air in commercial kitchens.

Expansion joint: A cut that is made or a gap that is deliberately left between sections of building materials to allow for expansion and contractor of those materials. Examples of expansion joints are found in large expanses of stucco walls, in concrete driveways and garage slabs and in swimming pool decks and patio decks. Expansion joints that are trowelled into concrete when it is poured are also called control joints or cold joints. Since concrete frequently cracks, the cracks are supposed to occur at these joints to control the cracking from occurring elsewhere.

Exposure: A measure for roofing, usually in inches, of the amount the roof shake, tile, or shingle is exposed to the weather.

F: Fahrenheit.

FAU: Forced-air unit (central heating).

FLM: Flood level rim

FMC: Flexible metal conduit ("Greenfield").

FSD: Fire separation distance.

FT: Feet, foot.

Factory-built fireplace: A fireplace composed of listed factory-built components assembled in accordance with the terms of the listing to form the completed fireplace. The appliance must be suitable for solid fuel and be equipped with a listed and properly installed chimney.

Fan-assisted appliance: An appliance equipped with an integral mechanical means to either draw or force products of combustion through the combustion chamber and/or heat exchanger.

Fascia: The trim board that covers the edge of the rafters at a pitched roof. May also be incorporated with a gutter to collect rainwater from the roof.

Fastener: Generic category including nails, screws, bolts, or anchors—also see Connector.

Feeders: Conductors supplying panelboards other than service panels.

Filter fabric: A textile made of synthetic threads that allows water to pass through but keeps particles of soil from passing through. Used to wrap underground drainage pipes and placed underneath roadways in unstable soil areas.

Finish coat: Refers to the final coat of material to be applied to a House. Examples are stucco, paint, drywall texture, deck coatings and other materials that require more than one application before being complete.

Fireblock: These are very similar to draft stops in their location and purpose. Fireblocks are building materials placed between floors, between walls, in vent shafts, in soffit ceilings, and in chimney chases to retard the spread of fire through small, concealed spaces of the building..

Firebox: That portion of the fireplace where the fire is actually built.

Firestop: Until the early 1990s, this term was used for what today is called fireblocking. A penetration firestop assembly is a group of materials installed to resist free passage of flame through an assembly, typically around a duct, vent, or chimney passing through a rated ceiling, floor, or wall.

Fire separation distance: The distance measured perpendicular from the building face to the closest interior or to the centerline of a street, alley, or public way.

Fixture branch drain: A drain serving two or more fixtures that discharges to another drain or to a stack.

Fixture branch supply: A water supply pipe between the fixture supply pipe and the water-distributing pipe.

Fixture drain: A drain from a fixture trap to a junction with any other drain; also called a trap arm.

Fixture unit: A unit of measure for the drain (DFU) or water supply (WSFU) load from different fixtures.

Flame safeguard: A device that will automatically shut off the fuel supply to a main burner or group of burners when the means of ignition of those burners becomes disabled and when flame failure occurs.

Flapper valve: The rubber or plastic valve at the bottom of the toilet tank that keeps the water in the tank until the flush level is pushed.

Flashing: Strips of material, usually metal, that are used to direct water and wind from one surface to another. Flashing is placed where a roof and a wall intersect. It is also placed around the intersection of chimneys and roofs, as well as where roof planes come together and where trim pieces often protrude from walls. Walls that terminate without being under a roof, such as a parapet, are flashed with cap flashing. Sometimes two flashing components work together, when one piece of flashing slides underneath the other; this is called counter-flashing.

Flatwork: A broad-based term referring to concrete placement that is flat. Examples include driveways, patios and walkways.

Flexibility after installation: Anticipated movement after initial installation, such as that caused by motor vibration or equipment repositioning.

Flood level rim: The level at which water overflows from a fixture or the surface to which it is fastened.

Flue: The pipe protruding from the top of the firebox, furnace, water heater, or other gas fired appliance that carries the hot burned gases to the atmosphere and outside the House. The term is also used as a substitute for "vent".

Flue collar: The outlet of an appliance designed for the attachment of a draft hood, vent connector, or venting system.

Flue gases: Products of combustion plus excess air in appliance flues or heat exchangers.

Flush: To be in the same plane or level with another object.

Forced draft: A vent system using a fan or other mechanical means to expel flue gases under positive static vent pressure.

Foundation: The lower most structural element of the House that supports the weight of the House. There are two primary foundation types: the raised footing and the slab on grade. There are also several variations of the two primary foundation types:
- **Basement:** These foundations are a form of grade beam foundation, since the basement wall becomes the grade beam. Basement walls are founded on perimeter footing and a slab is poured between the footings to complete the basement floor.
- **Conventional slab:** This refers to the method of reinforcing a building slab. Steel bars, called rebar, are crisscrossed to form a mat over which concrete is poured. In some cases, the reinforcing may be welded wire mesh.
- **Footing:** A term given to the underside of the grade beam or the underside of the edge of a slab. To provide additional foundation stability, foundations are made wider than the grade beam itself, and deeper than the thickness of the slab.
- **Grade beam:** Concrete is poured in a form to allow a first floor framing of the House to occur at least 6 inches higher than the surrounding ground. The grade beams comprise the exterior perimeter of the House and sometimes the interior grade beams are also poured to support bearing walls.
- **Piers:** Piers are holes drilled into the ground typically between 6 and 18 feet deep, reinforced with steel rods known as rebar, and filled with concrete. Piers are typically connected to the underside of grade beams. Less frequently, piers independently support the underside of houses. Even less frequently, piers are connected to the underside of slabs where unstable soil conditions warrant. The purpose of a pier is to provide additional stability to a foundation against upward and downward pressure.

- **Post tension slab:** A method of reinforcing where cables are crisscrossed in the slab area prior to pouring concrete. After the concrete is cured, the cables are tightened under extreme tension to provide a tight and dense foundation.
- **Slab on grade:** Where the concrete is poured on top of the finished and prepared lot that is ready to receive the concrete. Hence the concrete slab becomes the first floor of the House. Slab foundations can also have grade beams poured underneath them.

Frame: The frame is the skeleton of the house. It contains the elements to support the weight of the house as well as defining the shape of the house. The frame and the foundation are the most important structural components of the house.

Furnace: A mechanical device located in, around, or under the house, or sometimes in the attic, that is powered by either gas (natural or bottled), electricity, or fuel oil or a combination of sources of power. The furnace provides a source of heat for the house.

GAL: Gallons.

GB: Gypsum board.

GEC: Grounding electrode conductor.

GES: Grounding electrode system.

GFCI: Ground-fault circuit interrupter.

GFPE: Ground-fault protection of equipment.

GPF: Gallons per flush.

GPM: Gallons per minute.

Garage door: See Doors, garage.

Gas connector: Tubing or piping that connects the gas supply piping to the appliance.

Gooseneck: A curve at the top of a service entrance cable designed to prevent water from entering the open end of the cable.

Grade: A term denoting the elevation of a particular lot above sea level and the degree of levelness of that lot adjoining the building at all exterior walls. Finished grade is the finished ground level, or elevation of the lot (sometimes known as the pad) after the grading operations have been completed. A slab on grade is a foundation that has been poured on the finished grade. Grade is also a term used to described the type, quality, and strength of lumber that is used in the frame of a house.

Grain: The lines of harder and darker wood that run thought the field of a piece of lumber.

Greenboard: A special type of drywall that has moisture resistant characteristics. Its common application is basically seen around tubs and showers. Typically, it is either green or blue in color.

Ground: The earth.

Grounded conductor: A current-carrying conductor that is intentionally connected to earth (a neutral).

Grounding Electrode Conductor (GEC): A conductor used to connect the service neutral or the equipment to a grounding electrode or to a point on the grounding electrode system.

Ground fault: A unintentional connection of a current-carrying conductor to equipment, earth, or conductors that are not normally intended to carry current.
- **GFCI, Ground-Fault Circuit Interrupter:** A device to protect against shock hazards by interrupting current when an imbalance of 6 milliamps or more is detected. Areas that are subject to moist or wet conditions such as kitchens, baths, garages, and outdoor areas must have their electrical outlets connected to a ground fault interrupter.
- **GFPE, Ground-Fault Protected Equipment:** A device to protect equipment from ground faults and allowing higher levels of leakage current than a GFCI.

Grout: Material, usually containing cement, sand, or a plastic polymer material, and a coloring agent, which is placed between pieces of tile or marble. The joints between pieces of tile or marble are called grout joints. Stonework can also be grouted. Grout is also used to fill voids under foundation sills.

Gusset: A triangular piece of material often made of wood, plastic or metal, which is used to strengthen intersecting corners. Gussets are used inside hollow core doors and inside cabinet frames.

Gutter: An open linear collector and distributor of water. Gutters may be found at the eaves of roofs, or can be associated with curbs and sidewalks in streets and parking areas. Another possible location for gutters is in the middle of driveways and streets.

Gypsum: A powdery mineral that is white in color, non-combustible, and is primary ingredient in indoor plaster and drywall.

Gypsum board: See drywall.

HP: Horsepower (33,000 lb. ft/minute) or heat pump.

HR: Hour.

HRV: Heat-recovery ventilator.

H.S.P.F.: Heating seasonal-performance factor.

HVAC: An acronym standing for Heating, Ventilating and Air Conditioning. Refers to the specialty work of contractors who install furnaces, fans, air conditioning systems and sometimes other sheet metal items such as flashing, gutters and downspouts.

Habitable space: Space in a building for living, sleeping, eating, or cooking. Bathroom, bathroom closets, hallways, storage, or utility areas are not considered habitable space.

Hangers: See "supports".

Hardboard: A general term used to describe a variety of simulated wood products that are used primarily as exterior siding.

Hard water: Water that is high in mineral content mainly compounds of calcium and magnesium. Hard water restricts soap from lathering, and it can form deposits inside water lines and water heaters.

Header: A structural framing member made of wood or steel that spans the opening over a window or door.

Heart (heartwood): A term referring to the grade of lumber, usually redwood. Heartwood is from the inner core of the tree trunk. It is considered the best lumber because it is more uniform in appearance. The opposite of heartwood is sapwood. The term "sap wood" refers to the lumber that is milled from the outer-most portion of the tree. Sapwood is usually lighter in color than heartwood.

Hearth: The floor area with the fire chamber of a fireplace or fireplace stove.

Hearth extension: The surfacing applied to the floor area in front of and to the sides of the hearth opening of a fireplace or fireplace stove.

Heat pump: A system that utilizes the change of state of a refrigerant to extract heat from one substance and transfer it to another area of the same of different substance. Heat pumps can provide both heating and cooling.

Heat-recovery ventilator: A combination ventilation system that replaces indoor air with outdoor air that passes through a heat exchanger. The heat exchanger tempers the outdoor air to minimize energy losses. HRVs that also remove humidity from the indoor air are referred to as energy-recovery ventilators.

Hertz: A measure of the frequency of AC. In North America, the standard frequency is 60 Hertz.

Hold-downs: Structural metal straps that are embedded in the foundation at the time of pouring concrete and then are nailed to the framing members during construction. Hold-downs can also be compromised of anchor bolts, threaded rods, and metal gussets to tie the frame to the foundation in the event of an earthquake or loads (forces) caused by wind.

Holidays: A small area that the painter has missed or covered very lightly. Derived from the saying "it looks like the painter took a holiday."

Horizontal: Any pipe or vent, etc. that is less than 45° from horizontal.

Horizontal branch drain: A drainage pipe that extends from a stack or drain and that serves two or more fixtures.

Hot water: Water at a temperature 110°F (120°F in the UPC).

Heating seasonal-performance factor: The measure of a system's efficiency in heating mode. The higher the number, the more efficient the system.

IBC: International Building Code.

ICF: Insulating concrete form.

IMC: Intermediate metal conduit.

IN: Inch, inches.

IRC: International Residential Code.

Impermeable: The term given to the ability of a material to resist the passage of liquid through it. A plastic sheet or membrane that will not pass water is considered impermeable. Semi-permeable membranes allow for the passage of some moisture.

Individual branch circuit: see branch circuit, individual.

In sight: see within sight.

Indirect-fired water heater: a water heater with a storage tank equipped with a heat exchanger used to transfer heat from an external source to heat potable water. The storage tank could derive its heat source from an external source, such as solar or a boiler, or an internal source.

Indirect waste pipe: A waste discharge into the drainage system through an airbreak into a trap, fixture, or receptor, such as a clothes washer standpipe.

Individual vent: A pipe that vents a fixture trap.

Induced draft appliance: An appliance that utilizes a fan to overcome resistance of a heat exchanger and to assist in the delivery of flue gases to the appliance outlet (flue collar). Induced draft appliances typically deliver the flue gases to the flue collar at non-positive pressure due to the temperature of those gases relative to outside atmosphere. See "vented gas appliance categories."

Induced draft burner: A burner that depends upon a draft that is induced by a fan that is integral to the appliance and is downstream from the burner.

Insulation: A material used in the homebuilding industry that keeps a house from either gaining or losing heat. Normally insulation is put into the walls, under the bottom floor, and into the attic space during construction. Sometimes insulation is placed on the outside of slab foundations and is attached to the outer face of the studs before applying the exterior finish.

Interface: A point where two or more functions interact. For example, the telephone service company wiring meets and interacts with the house telephone wiring at a box called the interface.

Interrupting Rating: The highest current a breaker or fuse can interrupt without sustaining damage.

Jack: Has four meanings in homebuilding. The first refers to the metal assembly on the roof through which the plumbing vents and furnace flues run. The jack may be a combination of metal and a rubber gasket to ensure a watertight seal. The second use of the term jack refers to a screw device that can remedy certain out of level conditions on foundation and floor frame members. The third definition applies to a "phone jack", or the wall plate into which the phone cord is plugged. The fourth refers to any short filler in roof or wall plate into which the phone cord is plugged. The fourth refers to any short filler in roof or wall framing such as "jack rafter" or "jack stud".

Jamb: The stationary component of a door assembly to which the hinges are attached. The door assembly (excluding the door itself) is comprised of a jamb, stop, and casing.

Joint: Connection between two pipes.
- **Brazed joint:** Any joint obtained by joining metal parts with allows that melt at temperatures >840°F, but lower than the melting temperature of the parts to be joined.
- **Expansion joint:** A loop, return bend, or return offset that accommodates pipe expansion and contraction.
- **Flexible joint:** A joint that allows movement of one pipe without deflecting the other pipe.
- **Mechanical joint:** A joint that uses compression to seal the joint.
- **Slip joint:** A joint that incorporates a washer or special packing material to create a seal.

- **Soldered joint:** A joint obtained by a joining of metal parts with metallic mixtures or allows that melt at a temperature <800°F & >300°F.
- **Welded joint or seam:** Any joint or seam obtained by the joining of metal parts in the plastic molten state.

Joist: The horizontal members of the house frame that are the most common elements of a floor or ceiling system. While joists are the most common element of the floor system, other horizontal members known as beams or girders can also make up the floor system. Common joists have one nominal dimension, typically at 2 inches and the other nominal dimension at 8 inches, 10 inches, 12 inches, or 14 inches, depending upon how far they span. It is common practice today to use a manufactured component as a joist. This is called a truss; it is comprised of wood, metal or a combination of both. If a truss is used, it has been manufactured in a factory and approved for use by a structural engineer.

K: 1,000 (1kBtu=1,000Btu).

Kcmil: 1,000 circular mil units (conductor size).

KS: Kitchen sink.

Knocked down: A style of finished wall texture that is applied coarsely with a texture spray gun. The bumpy surface is then "knocked down" with a large metal straight edge known as a texture knife.

L&L: Listed and labeled.

LAV: Lavatory sink.

LB: Pound, pounds.

LP: Liquefied petroleum (LP gas).

LFMC: Liquidtight flexible metal conduit, a.k.a "Sealtight".

LFNMC; Liquidtight flexible nonmetallic conduit.

LT: Laundry tub.

Label: A marking applied on a product and that identifies the manufacturer, the function of designation of the product, and the agency that has evaluated a sample of that product.

Labeled: Equipment, materials, or products affixed with a label or other identifying mark to attest that the product complies with identified standards or has been found suitable for a specific purpose. See "listed".

Latch: That portion of the doorknob assembly that protrudes out from the door and upon closing the door fits into the hole provide by the strike. The term can also generically refer to any part of a door, gate or opening mechanism that hooks in a receptacle designed to receive it.

Lath: A material to which plaster is applied. Lath is usually metal in the form of wire or mesh that is applied over building paper to the exterior of the house prior to plastering. The lath provides a surface for the plaster to hang onto during its wet application, and lath reinforces plaster much in the same way rebar reinforces concrete. Prior to the wide spread use of drywall, interior house walls were plastered with gypsum plaster. The lath used behind this type of plaster was long strips of wood.

Ledger: A horizontal piece of lumber or steel used to support joists and rafters. The wood ledger, which is at least 2 inches nominal thickness, may support the joists y having them sit on top of the ledger or hand from the face of the ledger by metal brackets known as joists hangers. The most common application for the ledger is in the construction of a deck attached to the outside of the house.

Lighting outlet: An outlet intended for the direct connection of a lampholder or a luminaire.

Liquefied petroleum (LP) gas: LP or propane gas is composed primarily of propane, propylene, butanes, or butylenes or mixtures thereof that are gaseous under normal atmospheric conditions but are capable of being liquefied under moderate pressure at normal temperatures. LP gas is typically stored in tanks on site. Unlike natural gas (CH_4), LP gas (C_3H_8) is heavier than air.

Liquid waste: A discharge from any fixture or appliance that does not receive fecal matter.

Listed: Equipment or materials on a list published by an approved organization that is concerned with product evaluation and that maintains periodic inspection of production of listed equipment or materials. The listing will state that the product meets specified standards or has been found suitable for a specific purpose.

Live loads: Loads produced by use and occupancy of the building and not including wind, snow, rain, earthquake, flood, or dead loads.

Load: The demand on an electrical circuit measured in amps or watts.

Location, damp: An area protected from the weather, yet subject to moderate degrees of moisture, such as a covered porch.

Location, dry: A location not normally subject to dampness or wetness.

Location, wet: All areas subject to direct saturation with water, and all conduits in wet outdoor locations or underground or in concrete or masonry in earth contact.

Log lighter, gas-fired: A manually operated solid-fuel ignition device for installation in a vented solid-fuel burning fireplace. These are intended to help initiate a fire in a fireplace, as compared to a decorative appliance for installation in a fireplace.

Low-pressure hot-water heating boiler: A boiler furnishing hot water at pressures not exceeding 160psi or temperatures not exceeding 250°F.

Low-pressure steam-heating boiler: A steam boiler that operates at pressures not exceeding 15psi.

Luminaire (formerly lighting fixture): A complete lighting unit including parts to connect it to the power supply, and possibly parts to protect or distribute the light source. A lampholder, such as a porcelain socket, is not itself a luminaire.

MANU: Manufacturer

MAX: Maximum.

MC: Metal-clad cable.

MIN: Minimum.

MP: Medium pressure.

MPH: Miles per hour.

Makeup air: Air provided to replace air being exhausted.

Membrane: A thin sheet of material used to prevent the passage of water vapor into an area that would be damaged by water. Often used under deck surfaces.

Millwork: Refers to house components that are generally part of the interior finish of the house, and which are manufactured in a mill or shop, rather than constructed at the site of the house. Examples of millwork are cabinets and doors.

Miter cut: A method of cutting wood (usually trim pieces) at an angle other than 90 degrees so as to conceal the joint when the pieces of wood are placed together. Corner pieces of trim such as door casings and baseboards are often miter cut so that the cut end is not visible.

Monolithic: Concrete cast in one continuous operation with no joints, such as a footing and floor slab or a footing and foundation stem wall.

Mortar: Mortar is a mixture of sand and cement and may be used for setting brick, stonework, and preparing a bed upon which tile is set. Unlike concrete, mortar does not have aggregate (smooth rocks of various sizes, up to about ¾ inch). Grout is a form of mortar.

MP regulator: A line pressure regulator that reduces gas pressure from a medium pressure to a range at which appliances can utilize it (typically 0.5psig). These are often found in CSST systems with a central manifold.

Mudsill: The 2x4 or 2x6 section of lumber that is bolted to the foundation as the very first framing member. It must be pressure treated or foundation grade redwood.

Mullion: A strip that divides, or appears to divide, the panes of glass in a window. With many dual pane windows, a faux mullion is placed in the dead air space between the panes of glass.

NEC: National Electrical Code.

NFPA: National Fire Protection Association.

NM: Nonmetallic-sheathed cable.

Nationally Recognized Testing Laboratory (NRTL): A testing facility recognized by OSHA as qualified to provide testing and certification of products and services. Examples of NRTLs are CSA, NDF, and UL.

Natural-draft burner: A burner where proper combustion depends upon establishing a draft of flue gasses that will rise by the pressure difference between the flue gases and outside atmosphere.

Natural gas: Gas, usually odorized methane, supplied to the site by a gas utility company and metered at the site. Natural gas is lighter than air.

Negative slope: A slope or grade that runs in the wrong direction, causing water to flow opposite of the direction that is intended (see slope).

Neutral conductor: The conductor connected to the neutral point of a system that is intended to carry current under normal conditions.

Noncombustible material: Material that passes a test procedure as set forth in ASTM E136 for defining noncombustibility of materials. This includes materials that will not ignite and burn when subjected to fire, or material having a structural base of noncombustible material with a surfacing material not over 1/8in thick that has a flame-spread index not higher than 50. This does not apply to surface-finish materials, the entire material of which must be noncombustible from the standpoint of clearances to heating appliances.

O.C.: On center.

OCPD: Overcurrent protection device (breaker or fuse).

OSB: Oriented strand board.

Offset: A combination of elbows or bends in a line of piping that brings a section of the pipe out of line, but into a line parallel with the other section.

Open conductors: Individual conductors not contained within a raceway or cable sheathing, such as a typical service drop.

Ordinary tightness: Buildings of ordinary tightness are those that do not meet the standards for "unusually tight construction".

Oriented strand board: A manufactured wood product that comes in sheets that are 4 feet wide by 8, 9, or 10 feet in length. It can be part of the house frame on the subfloor, walls, or roofs. It is always covered by the finish flooring, siding, or roofing material.

Outlet: The point on a wiring system at which current is taken to supply equipment. A receptacle or a box for a lighting fixture is an outlet; a switch is not an outlet.

Overcurrent: Any current in excess of the rating of equipment or conductor insulation. Overcurrents are produced by overloads, ground faults, or short circuits.

Overfusing: A fuse or breaker that has an overload rating greater than allowed for the conductor it is protecting.

Overhead door: See Doors, garage.

Overload: Equipment drawing current in excess of the equipment or conductor rating and in such a manner that damage would occur if it continued for a sufficient length of time. Short circuits and ground faults are not overloads.

PE: Polyethylene tubing.

PEX: Crossed-link polyethylene tubing.

PL: Property line.

PP: Polypropylene plastic tubing.

PRV: Pressure relief valve.

PT: Pressure treated.

PSF: Pounds per square foot.

PSI: Pounds per square inch.

PSIG: Pounds per square inch gage.

PV: Photovoltaic.

PVC: A plastic pipe made from polyvinyl chloride. The most extensive use of this pipe is for irrigation supply lines. Other uses include storm and sewer piping. If the manufacturer adds another step to the process, called CPVC, the pipe can be used for cold-water household use in most locations.

Pad: A term given to the flat spot on a graded lot where the condominium or house is to be built. A padded lot refers to a lot that has been graded flat in one or more elevations and usually certified by a civil engineer. It is also the material installed under the carpet.

Panelboards: The "guts" of an electrical panel; the assembly of bus bars, terminal bars, etc., designed to be placed in a "cabinet." What is commonly called an electrical panel or load center is, by NEC terms, a panelboard mounted in a cabinet.

Parapet: A low wall that extends above the edge of a roof and often found on the sides of decks and balconies.

Particle board: A mixture of wood chips, sawdust and a glue-like binder called resin for creation of a synthetic wood product. It is manufactured in boards like lumber, or sheets like plywood, and has a broad range of applications in residential construction. Examples are shelving, door cores, and backing (underlayment) for tile and vinyl flooring. A related product, called oriented strand board (OSB), is used as roof underlayment and shear panels.

Patio: See Flatwork.

Pavers: Pieces of stone, concrete, or brick that are placed side-by-side to form walkways and driveways. Shapers can be square, rectangular, hexagonal or other geometric shapes. Depending on the specific use, pavers are set over a base of sand, concrete, or mortar.

Penny: A measurement of the size of nails. Derived from Old English where copper was used for both pennies and nails.

Perforated pipe: Pipe that has holes or slots through the sidewall of the pipe to permit the collection of subterranean drainage water of the discharge of wastewater in a septic tank system leach field.

Perm: The unit of measurement of water vapor transmission through a material based on the number of grains of water vapor at a given pressure differential. Vapor retarders are rated in perms.

PEX tubing: Water-supply tubing made of cross-linked polyethylene, typically found in parallel distribution systems. PEX-AL-PEX has a thin layer of aluminum sandwiched between layers of PEX. The aluminum serves as an oxygen barrier and helps overcome the bending memory of the PEX.

Pier: A column of concrete that extends down into the ground and is often attached to the underside of the grade beam. Sometimes an "independent" pier may be attached to the underside of the subfloor joists in the crawl space. The purpose of the pier is to provide additional load carrying capacity to the foundation.

Pitch: Also known as slope, the amount of drop (or rise) of a building component such as a roof, or deck. For example a roof that has 5 and 12 pitch means that for every 12 feet of horizontal measurement the roof would rise up 5 feet in vertical measurement.

Plain concrete or masonry: Structural concrete or masonry with less reinforcement than the minimum amount specified for reinforced concrete.

Plant on: An architectural feature that is usually glued to or fastened to the exterior of a house to add dimension and character to walls and windows. Used frequently in stucco applications.

Plaster: See Stucco.

Plumb: A term given to a wall that is perfectly straight up and down. Out of plumb means that the wall is titled to some measured extent.

Plenum: A chamber, other than the occupied space being conditioned, that forms part of the air circulation system

Plumbing system: The water-supply system, drainage system, storm drains, sewers, connected fixtures, supports, appurtenances, and appliances.

Ponding: A condition where flat surfaces that are supposed to drain collect water in depressed areas called ponds (also called birdbaths).

Post: A vertical structural element larger than a stud used in the framing of a house. Posts are usually the vertical support for horizontal beams. Posts can also be found as a component in handrails.

Potable water: Water fit for human consumption.

Pot shelf: An architectural feature found on the inside and outside of some houses, used to permit the placement of pots. Often found in hallways and in bedrooms above closets, as well as on the exterior in front of windows.

Power: There are 2 designations for AC electrical power. Apparent power (input) is expressed in V x A. true power (useful output) is expressed in watts.

Power vent: See "forced draft".

Pre-emergent: A chemical that is applied to landscape areas in winter and spring prior to the growth of weeds to prevent weed seeds from sprouting.

Pressure-balancing valve: A mixing valve that senses incoming hot and cold water pressures and compensates for fluctuations in either to stabilize outlet temperature. They can be built into shower and tub mixers or added as separate devices ahead of other individual fixtures.

Pressure boundary: The boundary separating indoor from outdoor air. A ventilated crawlspace or attic would be outside the pressure boundary.

Pressure relief valve: A device designed to protect against high pressure and to function as a relief mechanism.

Pressure treated: A chemical treatment given to lumber that may or will come in contact with the earth (ground). The process often gives a greenish or brownish color to the wood and linear perforations ("pickling marks") on the sides. Mudsills and fence posts are examples of lumber that should be pressure treated.

Primer: Refers to the base coat or initial coat of a liquid, usually paint, sometimes resin, which penetrates and adheres to the coated object and provides a compatible surface for finish coats.

Public sewer: A sewer controlled by a public authority

Public water main: Water supply pipe controlled by public authority.

REQ: Require.

REQ'D: Required.

REQ'S: Requires, requirements.

RMC: Rigid Metal Conduit.

R-Value: The measurement of the ability of a substance to gain or lease heat. Insulation is rated by its R-value. The higher the R-Value (like R-11, R-22, R-38, etc), the greater ability to insulate.

Rafter: The common structural lumber used to create the frame of roof. The rafters define the shape of the roof as well as the slope.

Readily accessible: Access that does not require removing a panel or door. For electrical equipment, this also means not having to resort to use of a ladder.

Rebar: The steel rods that are placed in a form, such as a foundation, to give added strength and resistance to prevent concrete cracking.

Reduced-pressure principle backflow preventer (RPPBP): An RPPBP consists of two independently acting check valves, internally pressure forced to the normally open position. These checks are separated by an intermediate chamber that is equipped with a means of automatic relief. Should there be a reversal of flow, the downstream liquid will drain instead of placing backpressure on the supply liquid. RPPBPs have a means of field testing.

Refractory: A term given to ceramic or brick like material that is made to withstand heat. Many fireplaces have precast panels of refractory material at the sides and back.

Relief vent: A vent providing air circulation between vent and drainage systems.

Rim: An unobstructed open edge of a fixture.

Riser: The vertical, back piece of a stair step that separates on tread from another.

Roof: The upper most structural component of the house or the building frame. A number of other terms are associated with roofs:

- **Gable:** A simple design of pitched roofs having a high point (called the ridge) and a low point (at the eave).
- **Hip:** A gable roof that has been clipped back at its outer end, and with a sloped roof added to the clipped area.
- **Mansard:** A small, steeply pitched portion found around the perimeter of low pitched or flat roofs as an element of architectural enhancement.
- **Rake:** The line of the roof running from the ridge to the eave. Rakes can occur at the ends of gables, or where two sections of roof join in a hip.
- **Ridge:** The highest horizontal part of the roof.
- **Shed:** A pitched roof where the upper most part terminates at a well, or a pitched roof that starts at the top of a wall and is pitched only one direction (as opposed to a gable roof which is pitched in two directions).
- **Valley:** The opposite of **hip** (see above definition). The low point where two roof planes intersect.

Roof Cover: While the roof is part of the house of building structure, the roof cover is the material that gives the water shedding or water repellency nature to the roof. Examples of roof covers are noted:

- **Asphalt composition or shingle:** Made primarily by combining fiberglass or felt with a petroleum product and finishing the outer surface with granulated sand, stone, or other hard substance. Applied in strips about 3 feet long.
- **Built-up roof:** Also known as low pitch or flat roofs. The most common material used in this type of roof is hot asphalt (tar) mopped over a felt membrane and covered with gravel. Other materials used include rubber sheeting and elastomeric coatings.
- **Tile:** A term given to individual pieces made from mortar (called concrete) or terra cotta. The material can be colored in the manufacturing process and it comes glazed or unglazed. Shapes include flat pieces (known as shakes), interlocking "S" shapes, or semicircular barrels.
- **Wooden shake or wooden shingle:** Usually made from split cedar logs and hand applied on the roof one at a time.
- **Other:** There are numerous other roof coverings that have limited use in new house construction. These include metal shingles with

granular material glued on them, shakes made of cement and fiberglass, and reconstituted wood shakes.

Room heater, circulating: A room heater with an outer jacket surrounding the heat exchanger, and with openings at the top and bottom designed to circulate air between the heat exchanger and outer jacket.

Room heater (liquid or gas fuel): A room heater installed in the space to be heated and not connected to a duct.

Room heater, radiant: A room heater designed to transfer heat primarily by direct radiation.

Room heater (solid fuel): A solid-fuel-burning appliance designed to operate with the fire chamber door closed. See *"fireplace stove."*

Room large in comparison to size of equipment: A room having at least 12 times the volume of a furnace or other air-handling device, or 16 times the volume of a boiler. When the ceiling is greater than 8ft, the volume is calculated based upon an 8ft height. See *"alcove."*

Rosette: The two circular end pieces (usually plastic) mounted on the sidewall of a closet. The purpose of a rosette is to provide the niche into which the closet pole is inserted. Also a rosette is the round portion of the door hardware used to trim out the hole boarded through the door.

Rough-in: Part of the plumbing system that is installed in a structure before fixture installation.

SCCR: Short circuit current rating.

SDC: Seismic Design Category.

SE: Service entrance cable.

SFD: Single-family dwelling.

SQ.: Square, as in sq. ft.

Scalloping: An unacceptable condition of finished boards (including flooring) where the saw has made irregular cuts or chips out of the surface of the board.

Screw drive: The method of operation of some garage door opener mechanisms. Also known as worm drive. The screw drive is a long steel rod that runs between the opener and the door header and it revolves in a clockwise and counterclockwise direction.

Scupper: An opening in the outside edge of a low slope roof or deck to allow rainwater to pass from the roof or deck over the side.

Seismic: A term frequently used in conjunction with earthquake activity. Seismic design, i.e. making the house stronger and less prone to damage in an earthquake, is a part of the Building Code. Some seismic building methods include tying the house to the foundation with long metal straps and using shear panels to keep the house from moving back and forth during an earthquake.

Seismic Design Category (SDC): Classification assigned to buildings based upon located and severity of earthquake ground motion expected at the site.

Service: The conductors and equipment providing a connection to the utility.

Service drop: The overhead conductors supplied by the utility.

Service entrance conductors: The conductors from the service point to the service disconnect.

Service equipment: The equipment at which the power conductors entering the building can be switched off to disconnected the premises' wiring from the utility power source. A meter can be a part of or separate from the service equipment.

Service lateral: Underground service entrance conductors.

Service point: The connection or splice point at which the service drop and service entrance meet—it is the handoff between the utility and the customer.

Sewage: Liquid waste that contains chemicals or animal or vegetable matter.

Sewage ejector: A device for lifting sewage at high velocity with air or water.

Sewage pump: A device, other than an ejector, for lifting sewage from a sump.

Sheathing: The part of the roof that covers the rafters. Sheathing is usually plywood or a wood type of product. Strip sheathings are strips of 1x3 inch of 1x4 inch boards that are nailed across the rafters to provide a nailing surface for shingles and shakes.

Sheetrock: See Drywall.

Shielded coupling: An approved elastomeric sealing gasket with an approved outer shield and a tightening mechanism (i.e., no hub coupling).

Short circuit: A direct connection of current-carrying conductors without the interposition of a load, resulting in high levels of current.

Short Circuit Current Rating (SCCR): The amount of current that panelboards and switchboards must be able to carry during a short circuit condition without sustaining damage. See *interrupting rating*.

Shower pan: The bottom part of a shower. It may have been installed as a single unit or tiled over a waterproofing system.

Siding: The exterior covering of a house. Many materials can be used for siding, including wood, brick, vinyl, aluminum, plaster (stucco), and cement board.

Sill: The bottom of a window or patio door that is often confused with the trim piece, known as the stool, which is placed on the sill. Another sill, known as the mudsill, is the first piece of horizontal framing that is boiled to the foundation. Mudsills are required to be of termite resistant wood.

Slab: A term given to flat concrete and is often used with a foundation type known as slab on grade; also used in reference to the floor of a garage or basement known as the garage slab and basement slab.

Slope: Sometimes also referred to as pitch or "fall". The percentage or angle that a surface (such as a patio, driveway, or the grading around the house) drops, as one moves outward from the house. When dealing with plumbing pipes the term "fall" is used, which means the percentage or degree of inclination of the pipe.

Snap switch: A typical wall switch, including 3-way and 4-way switches.

Soffit: An architectural term given to a roof projection that has had the underside enclosed so that the rafters cannot be seen. Overhead decks and walkways may be constructed in a manner so as to have soffits.

Soil pipe: A pipe that conveys waste including fecal matter.

Sole plate: The 2x4 or 2x6 (sometimes 4x4 or 4x6) section of lumber that is laid flat on the slab or subfloor and the wall studs are attached to the plate. In the case of concrete slab, the sole plate and the mudsill are the same.

Spalling: The chipping or flaking of the exterior surface of a building material, usually concrete, that deeply pits the surface of the material. Concrete is known to spall in cold climates where there is repeated wetting and freezing of the surface. Cement plaster (stucco) can also spall for the same reason. Spalling can also occur in concrete when it is allowed to dry out (cure) too quickly.

Spark arrester: A metal screen-like device that is mounted on top of the chimney to prevent hot ashes from passing into the atmosphere and creating a fire hazard.

Splash block: A shallow trough with one open end that is placed under the discharge of a downspout to direct rainwater away from the foundation. Splash blocks are usually made of cast concrete, but they can also be made of cast fiberglass and metal.

Spores: Microscopic organisms that are capable of rapid reproduction and give rise to a new adult molds, mildews, and fungi. Found in mushrooms, ferns, mosses, as well as other organic material.

Stack: A vertical drain line that extends one or more stories.

Stack vent: A vent that extends from a stack.

Stack venting: A method of venting fixtures through the soil or waste stack.

Static pressure: The pressure existing in a system without any flow.

Stile: The right and left side pieces of a door or cabinet that run from top to bottom.

Stool: The piece of trim that sits horizontally on the sill of a window – often accompanied with a companion piece underneath it known as an apron. "Stool" can also refer to the lower piece of a toilet. Two-piece toilets have a tank to hold the flushing water and a stool to receive the waste.

Stoop: A step, or series of steps, plus a landing that leads to the exterior doors of a house.

Storm collar: A piece of metal that looks like a clerical collar and is attached to the chimney cap or cent from a gas appliance. The flue runs through the storm collar.

Story: That portion of a building that is between the upper surface of one floor at below the upper surface of the next floor above or the roof.

Story above grade: That part of the building that is more than 6 feet above grade for more than 50% of the total building perimeter or more than 12 feet above ground at any point.

Strike: That portion of door and cabinet hardware that is attached to the frame and receives the latch (through a hole in it) when the door is closed.

Stringer: The side boards on either side of a stairway. Unless the stairway is open, the treads run from one stringer across to the other.

Stucco: The exterior surface of a house that has been applied by troweling or spraying, to comprise a hard weather resistant surface. Stucco can be a form of mortar; known as cement plaster (sand and cement) or it can be a more synthetic material consisting of plastic resins and materials to bind them together. Many final textures are available for stucco including skip trowel, sand float, and brocade.

Stud: The common vertical structural pieces, usually wood, sometimes steel, which support the walls of a house. Studs are mostly 2 inches x 4 inches in cross dimension, although sometimes they can be 2 inches x 6 inches.

Subdrain: A drain that is placed underground to catch and divert subsurface water.

Subfloor: The flat flooring material that is connected to the floor joists. It is often made of plywood or several plywood substitutes. The finish floor, such as carpet, hardwood, tile, or linoleum, covers from the subfloor.

Subpanel: A large electrical box with a metal or plastic door usually found mounted in the wall inside the house or garage. The subpanel contains the circuit breakers or fuses of the branch electrical circuits. Houses may have more than one subpanel. The main panel is the box on the outside of the house that contains the electric meter and possibly some circuit breakers.

Subsidence: See Displacement.

Subsurface water: Water that passes underground through the soil, usually from a distant source and may cause soil to slide and swell, creating stability problems for houses.

Sump: A tank or pit that receives waste and is discharged by mechanical means.

Supports: Devices used to support or secure pipes, fixtures, or equipment.

Swale: A surface path for seasonal water flow that can be natural or man-made. Often swales are cut around houses as part of the finished grading process to allow rainwater to flow away from the house and out toward the street.

Sweat: The process by which copper piping is joined together. Using a torch, the parts to be joined are heated and the solder flows into the joint. This process is known as "sweating" pipes.

Swing: Sometimes known as hand, the term describes whether a door swings to the right or the left as you face it and open it toward you. Left-hand doors open and swing to the left and right hand doors open and swing to the right. Swing is an important thing to know when replacing doorknobs.

TEMP: Temperature.

TPRV: Temperature & pressure relief valve.

Tack strip: A narrow strip of wood with specialized nails driven through it in the opposite direction of the anchor nails, designed to catch and hold the edge of carpet. Tack strips are about 1-inch wide and up to 8 feet long and are nailed to the subfloor or concrete floor around the perimeter of a room. Protruding through the wood strips are sharp ends of specialized tacks. These tacks grab the carpet backing as the carpet is stretched toward the wall.

Tailpiece: Pipe or tubing connecting the outlet of a plumbing fixture to a trap.

Tannins: A substance found in many plants and trees that is acidic and dark in color. Tannins will leach when the material is wetted or crushed. Two materials that contain significant tannins are redwood and oak wood.

Temperature & pressure relief valve: A device designed to protect against high pressure or temperature and to function as a relief for either.

Threshold: A piece of wood, metal, or plastic that is placed on the bottom of the exterior door opening to direct water away from the opening.

Tits (slang): Having all the required or desirable elements, qualities, or characteristics; as good as it is possible to be.

Toe kick: A small piece of wood at the bottom of cabinets, usually about 4 inches high, which lifts the cabinet off the floor and is recessed behind the cabinet face.

Ton (cooling): The amount of heat energy required to melt one ton of ice (288,000Btus). Air conditioners and heat pumps are typically sized in terms of tonnage, based on melting a ton of ice in one day. Therefore one ton of AC = 288,000Btus/24hrs =12,000Btus. The tonnage of a unit is usually encoded in the model number as a multiplier of 12, i.e., the number 36 would equal a 3-ton unit.

Top dip (of trap): See "Upper dip."

Townhouse: Single-family dwelling unit constructed in groups of three or more attached units in which each unit extends from foundation to roof and with a yard or public way on at least two sides.

Trap: The piece of waste pipe just below sinks (visible), and below tubs and showers (not visible), shaped like a "U" or a "P". Traps retain some of the wastewater and prevent sewer gases from backing into the house.

Trap arm: A horizontal pipe between a trap and the connection to the drain and vent system—also called a fixture drain.

Trap seal: Vertical distance between the crown weir and the upper dip of the trap.

Tread: The flat part of a step.

Trench Drain: A subterranean drainage trench that contains a perforated pipe at the bottom and is filled with a gravel mix. The term is often mistakenly interchanged with "French Drain" which is a gravel filled trench without the pipe.

Trim: A generic term given to material that "finishes off" or dresses up a house. Various examples of trim are baseboard, door casings, window stools and aprons, crown molding, wood applied to the exterior around windows, and material that is applied to the house (usually wood) after the stucco or siding has been installed.

Truss: A structural component that has been engineered and manufactured to carry the weight of a floor or weight of a roof. Trusses are often substituted for common floor joists and common rafters.

Tuckpoint: To use a pointed masonry trowel to make repairs on mortar joints.

Tubular basis: Traps, waste bends, and tailpieces with slip-joint connections.

UF: Underground feeder cable

UFER: A concrete-encased grounding electrode, named after the developer of the system, Herbert Ufer.

UL Label: A label affixed to electrical appliances that have passed the independent tests administered by Underwriters Laboratory.

USE: Underground service entrance cable.

Unconfined space: A room or space having at least 50 cu. ft. for each 1,000Btu of the fuel-burning appliances contained in the room or space.

Underlayment: Sheet of material, usually plywood, particleboard, or cement board that is placed underneath the product that covers them to give rigidity. Used in roofing and flooring applications. The underlayment, if coated, can serve as a membrane.

Unit switch: A switch that is an integral part of an appliance.

Unlisted: An appliance not shown to comply with nationally recognized standards by an approved testing agency. An unlisted appliance might still have nameplate instructions. The IRC does not accept unlisted appliances. The UMC leaves their acceptance to the AHJ.

Unusually tight construction: Construction with walls and ceilings having a vapor retarder of 1 perm or less with sealed or gasketed openings, weather-stripping on openable windows and doors, and caulking or sealant at joints. Buildings of unusually tight construction are required by many energy codes and have a targeted air infiltration rate <0.35 ACH.

Upper dip: Highest point in the internal cross section of the trap at the lowest part of the bend. By contrast, the bottom dip is the lowest point in the internal cross section.

Useful life: The term given to how long a particular component or product is supposed to last. Useful lives are provided by manufacturers, by insurance companies, and by industry groups based upon actual experience and testing. If a product becomes obsolete, but is not worn out, it is also said that its useful life has passed.

V: Volt, volts, such as a 120V circuit.

VA: Volt-amperes, units of apparent power.

Vapor barrier: A sheet membrane that has numerous applications to keep moisture from entering (or in some cases leaving) a house. Vapor barriers are installed on the exterior of the frame of a house prior to the application of siding or stucco. Building paper serves as a vapor barrier prior to the installation of lath and stucco. Concrete slabs are poured over a plastic vapor barrier to keep moisture in the ground moving up through the concrete via capillary action. In colder climates interior vapor barriers are put in the inside of exterior walls under the drywall to keep the humidity of the house at a constant level.

Vaulted ceiling: A ceiling that is not flat, but rather follows the pitch of the roof, or the underside of the truss.

Venner: A thin layer of finished material applied over a much thicker layer of core material. It is a common practice for door, cabinets, and furniture manufacturers to place a veneer of fine wood over a core of particle board as part of their manufacturing process. Veneers can also be brick or masonry products.

Vent (fuel-burning appliances): A passageway for conveying flue gases from an appliance to the outside atmosphere.

Vent (plumbing): A pipe or device for introduction of air into the plumbing system to equalize pressure, allow drainage, and prevent siphoning of trap seals.

Vent, type B: A vent listed & labeled for use with appliances with draft hoods and other Category I appliances.

Vent, type BW: A vent listed & labeled for use with wall furnaces.

Vent, type L: A vent listed & labeled for appliances requiring either type L (oil-fired appliance) vents or type B vents.

Vent connector: A device that connects an appliance to a vent.

Vent stack: A vertical vent pipe that provides air circulation for the drainage system.

Vented gas appliance categories:
- **Category I:** An appliance that operates with nonpostive vent static pressure and with a gas vent temperature that avoids excessive condensate production in the vent.
- **Category II:** An appliance that operates with nonpositive vent static pressure and a vent gas temperature that is capable of causing excessive condensate production in the vent.
- **Category III:** An appliance that operates with a positive vent static pressure and with a vent gas temperature that avoids excessive condensate production in the vent.
- **Category IV:** An appliance that operates with a positive vent static pressure and with a vent gas temperature that is capable of causing excessive condensate production in the vent.

Vents: There are many types of vents found in houses. Here are some of the more common ones:
- **Attic:** Attic vents are usually louvered, often round, and found underneath the gables of a roof. Attic vents allow heat to escape during summer months.
- **Foundation:** Foundation vents are installed with pier and grade beam foundations. These vents allow air to circulate and moisture to escape.
- **Plumbing:** Plumbing vents are pipes that stick up through the roof and allow wastewater to pass through the house plumbing without becoming air locked.
- **Soffit:** Vents that are found on the underside of soffits. They may be round, rectangular, or narrow and long.
- **Window:** That portion of the window that opens and closes is called the vent.
- **Other:** Examples of other vents are exhaust fans, water heater flues, and cooktop vents.

Vertical: Any pipe or vent, etc. that is 45° or more from horizontal.

W: Watts, units of true (useful) power.

W/: With.

W/O: Without.

WC: Water closet (toilet).

WH: Water heater.

WRB: Water-resistive barrier.

WSP: Wood structural panel.

WSFU: Water supply fixture unit.

Walkthrough: A practice used by Builders when a new house is delivered to the Homeowner. A representative of the Builder walks through the house with the Homeowner prior to delivery. Often the Builder will demonstrate the features of the house and give the Homeowner instructions on care and maintenance. This even is also a very important opportunity for the Homeowner to note any items that are not complete or appear to be unacceptable. For example, countertop scratches and marks on the walls will probably not be covered under a Builder's limited warranty once the Homeowner takes possession of the house.

Walkway: See Flatwork.

Wall: The exterior and interior vertical component system of a house. There are many types of walls and several examples are described here.

- **Bearing wall:** A wall that carries a portion of the weight of the house. Most exterior walls are bearing walls. Some interior walls are also bearing walls.
- **Headwall:** Not a wall in a house, but a wall that has been constructed as part of a storm drain channel or piping system. The headwall is the concrete wall that serves as the beginning of a system where rain and storm water will flow from a channel into a system of piping.
- **Nonbearing wall:** A wall that is partition between rooms, but does not carry the weight of any portion of the structure above it.
- **Party wall:** A wall where most likely two walls are constructed to separate one condominium from another or one townhouse from another. Also known as common walls, these walls must be constructed according to a specific standard in the Building Code.
- **Rated wall (ceiling):** A wall that has been constructed to meet certain fire resistive and noise transmission standards.
- **Shear wall:** A wall of a house that has been reinforced against back and forth movement (caused by earthquakes and wind forces) using sheets of plywood, oriented strand board, or other materials approved by the Building Code.

Waste: Liquid-borne waste free of fecal matter.

Waste pipe: A pipe that conveys only waste.

Water hammer: The action of water under high pressure, rushing through pipes and hitting a turn in the piping or a closed valve. Water hammer makes a hanging noise in the piping. It can eventually break the piping connections and cause the piping to come loose. A common water hammer problem is the electric valves on a washing machine closing quickly between cycles.

Water main: A water supply controlled by a public entity or utility.

Water pipe: A pipe that conveys water to fixtures and outlets.

Waterproofing: Materials that protect retaining walls, windows, certain stucco surfaces, or other building elements from the passage of moisture as either vapor or liquid under hydrostatic pressure.

Water supply fixture unit: A measure of the estimated normal demand on the water supply by various types of plumbing fixtures.

Water supply system: Pipes, valves, fittings, and supports that supply water to and throughout a residence & its accessories, such as sprinkler piping.

Water Table: A trim piece that runs horizontally along an exterior wall that separates two different types of finish materials, such as brick and siding.

Weatherstrpping: Material made of plastic, felt, rubber, and metal that is placed around the frames of doors and windows to provide a final seal against the intrusion of wind and rain.

Weep holes: A small hole found at the exterior side of most windows to allow rainwater to exit from the channel of the window onto the outside of the building.

Weep screed: A strip of metal, used as a part of stucco applications, running parallel to the ground, about 6 inches off the ground where the stucco terminates. Rainwater that may be trapped behind the stucco will run down the building paper and exit through the weep screed.

Weir: See *"Crown weir"*.

Wet vent: A vent that also serves as a drain.

Whirlpool bathtub (hydromassage tub): A bathtub fixture equipped & fitted with a pump and circulating piping and that is drained after each use. A spa is not a whirlpool tub.

Within sight (also written as "in sight"): Visible, unobstructed, and not more than 50ft. away.

Wood stove: See "fireplace stove" or "room heater (solid fuel)".

Wood structural panel (WSP): A panel manufactured from veneers (plywood) or wood strands (OSB) and bonded with waterproof synthetic resins. Wood structural panels must bear a grade stamp (see p.18) and are used in floors, roof diaphragms, and shear walls.

ZU: Zinc, galvanized.

BIBLIOGRAPHY AND REFERENCES

American Concrete Institute. (2011). *ACI 318-Building Code Requirements for Structural Concrete*. Farmington Hills, MI.

American Concrete Institute. (2011). *ACI 530- Building Code Requirements for Masonry Structures*. Farmington Hills, MI.

American Forest and Paper Association. (2011) *Wood Frame Construction Manual for One- and Two-Family Dwellings (WFCM)*. Leesburg, VA.

American Iron and Steel Institute. (2007). *Standard for Cold-Formed Steel Framing—Prescriptive Method for One - and Two-Family Dwellings (AISI S230)*. Washington D.C.

American Society of Heating, Refrigerating and Air-Conditioning Engineers. (2006-2009). *ASHRAE Handbook: Fundamentals*. Atlanta, GA.

Ballast, D. (1994). *Handbook of Construction Tolerances*. McGraw Hill.

Building Industry Association of San Diego County. (1993). *Top 25 Construction Problems and Their Resolution*. Construction Quality Task Force.

California Building Industry Association. (2005). *SB 800, The Homebuilder "FIX IT" Construction Dispute Resolution Law*. Sacramento, CA.

California, State of, Department of Real Estate. (1996). *Operating Cost Manual for Homeowner Association*. Sacramento, CA.

California, State of, Contractor's State License Board. (1982). *Workmanship Guidelines*. Sacramento, CA.

Concrete Committee of San Diego County. (2001). *Concrete Performance Standards and Maintenance guidelines*. San Diego, CA.

Gypsum Association. (2012). *Fire Resistance Design Manual*. Hyattsville, MD.

Hansen, D. & Kardon, R. (2011). *Code Check – Building*. Taunton Press. Newtown, CT.

Hansen, D. & Kardon, R. (2010). *Code Check – Electrical*. Taunton Press. Newtown, CT.

Hansen, D. & Kardon, R. (2011). *Code Check – Plumbing &Mechanical.* Taunton Press. Newtown, CT.

International Code Council. (2007). *California Building Code.* Whittier, CA.

International Code Council. (2007). *California Electrical Code.* Whittier, CA.

International Code Council. (2007). *California Mechanical Code.* Whittier, CA.

International Code Council. (2007). *California Plumbing Code.* Whittier, CA.

International Code Council. (2006-2009). *International Residential Code for One and Two Family Dwellings.* Washington D.C.

International Association of Plumbing & Mechanical Officials. (2009). *Uniform Mechanical Code.* Ontario, CA.

International Association of Plumbing & Mechanical Officials. (2009). *Uniform Plumbing Code.* Ontario, CA.

Journal of Light Construction. (1997). *Troubleshooting Guide to Residential Construction*, Builderburg Group.

NAHM Research Center, Inc. (2001). *Mold in Residential Buildings.* Washington D.C.

National Association of State Contracting Licensing Agencies. (2009). *NASCLA Residential Construction Standards.* Phoenix, AZ.

National Fire Protection Association. (2011). *National Electrical Code.*

National Roofing Contractor's Association. (2007-1009). *NCRA Roofing and Waterproofing Manual.* Vols 1, 2, & 3. Rosemont, IL.

National Wood Flooring Association. (2000). *Problems, Causes and Cures.* Ellisville, MO.

NAHB Home Builder Press. (2005). *Residential Construction Performance Guidelines.* Washington D.C.

New Jersey, State of, Division of Codes and Standards. (2005). *Homeowners booklet*, New Home Warranty Program. NJ.

Reynolds, D. (1998). *Residential & Light Commercial Construction Standards*. R.S. Means, Inc. Kingston, MA.

Sacks, A. (1994). *Residential Water Problems*. NAHM Home Builder Press. Washington, DC.

Structural Building Component Association & Truss Plate Institute. (2006-2013). *Guide to Good Practice for Handling, Installing, Restraining & Bracing of Metal Plate Connected Wood Trusses*.

Tenebaum, D. (1996). *The Complete Idiot's Guide to Trouble Free Home Repair*. Alpha Books. NY.

Truss Plate Institute. (2008). *National Design Standard for Metal Plate Connected Wood Truss Construction*. Alexandria, VA.

ABOUT THE AUTHOR

Ryan Brautovich is an Army veteran with more than 20 years of home construction, home remodeling and building experience who has consulted for Fortune 500 home builders as well as the Top 100 privately held home building companies. He is a custom home builder in California and a California licensed general contractor. Ryan is International Code Council Certified, an International and California Building Inspector as well as an International and California Plumbing Inspector. He is a graduate of Auburn University with degrees in both Accounting and Business Management. He has consulted for the City of Lancaster (CA) Building & Safety Department, K. Hovnanian Homes, Beezer Homes, Pardee Homes, KB Homes, Standard Pacific Homes, American Premiere Homes, Richmond American Homes, DR Horton, and Frontier Homes – just to name a few.

Ryan founded the Construction H.E.L.P. Foundation, a national nonprofit organization, dedicated to advocating for and meeting the needs of individuals who have suffered at the hands of unscrupulous contractors and sub-contractors who simply took advantage of the helpless homeowner in order to make a quick buck – and either didn't finish the project, over-charged or simply took money and didn't perform the work as promised. Over the years, the number of phone calls Ryan received increased dramatically from frustrated and angry homeowners who were desperately seeking help after being ripped off by other contractors. As a result, he founded the Construction H.E.L.P. Foundation, and it's educational assistance program – Home Construction Audit – to provide assistance and education to homeowners. As the founder of the Construction H.E.L.P. Foundation, Ryan has made it the organization's daily mission to return ethics to the home building and home remodeling profession and provide homeowners with the expert help and crucial knowledge they need so that they will never be taken advantage of again.

www.ingramcontent.com/pod-product-compliance
Lightning Source LLC
Chambersburg PA
CBHW020810160426
43192CB00006B/518